A Tune in a Blind Man's Ears
and Other Poems

Christopher Ryan Turpin

110 copies of this chapbook were printed by Paper Machine
in New Orleans & sewn by friends.
Book design by Geoff Munsterman
Woodblock illustration by Pilar Z. McCracken
All writings by Christopher Ryan Turpin

Introduction

As an Appalachian person, it has always been my sincere hope that the best parts of our culture would survive the homogenization that seems to be the goal of the academic and pop-culture worlds we live in. While I am not qualified by time or institution to make that decision for anybody else, I realized long ago that these beautiful dialects would die to time if someone did not take action. I made up my mind as a student at Brevard College that I would do all in my power to attempt to write within the parameters of the dialect I heard from the older people I grew up listening to. Many authors from our mountains and from the south have done this very well. It is my opinion that more have gilded much of that which, on its own, is already golden. This author hopes the reader will recite these poems as they are written and savor them.

If you are reading this, I appreciate your purchase of or interest in these poems. If this book was a gift, I hope you will treasure it. If you found it on a sidewalk or neglected somewhere, I hope you will count it a blessing; at the very least, you have decent kindling for a fire. Finally, let none of us be ashamed of where we come from. Whatever the shortcomings of a place or its people, we are the product of where we come from, regardless of where we find ourselves. I am grateful beyond words for you all and I thank you for your support of my work.

—Christopher R. Turpin

*To the elders, family and chosen family alike,
the people of Hiawassee, Georgia,
the old and young, living and dead of Appalachia,
and especially to my New Orleans family:
Daren and Elise Martin, Zack Frazier, Zach Mohr,
Bridey Murphy, Geoff and Shadow*

*and also my teachers, living and dead:
Melissa Bridges,
Irma and Tommy Flanagan, Jerry Taylor,
Dr. Betsy Burrows,
and Byron Herbert Reece.*

I

Th' sky hwas acryin fer you.
Hwhen th' sun started asset'n
Th' Maker wiped 'er face hweth clouds
An' lef no rainbow signs t'
Comfort ner hep it.

I'm amournin yet an' haint stopp'd.
These three days is th' longest life.
Like a small chil' robb'd 'f a man,
I hwant m' two dollars back
From off yer still eyes.

I didn' give you th' roses,
Honly m' life's breath hwhile you lived.
Th' ol ones sang 'Vain Worl' Adieu'.
Hwas it vain fer me t' love?
Hwas I vain t' you?

II

A gud flannel shirt
Worn as th' crow flies,
Cotton-made 'f th' har 'f
Th' cotillion debutants
'f Flor'da an' Alabamer,
Combed straight b' an arish March win',
Arned hot an' thin
An' beat b' th' switch 'f th' Summer
Staves off th' col' an' keeps you warm
An' stores hup th' sweat t' keep you cool.

Hef th' breeze blows as th' road runs,
Hit'll be a long day, boys.
Yuns can bet on that.

III

Now shore I'm a man
An' put away m' childish thangs.
A man's troubled min'
Has tuck th' place 'f toys an' sport.

I go t' th' church
Cause 'f m' raisin, shore I do.
Granny raised me right
An' wrote in m' Bible pages.

I read in scratches,
Lean on ever' jot an' tittle.
In m' darkest hours,
Er wrinkled tech still arrests fyear.

IV

She's too young t' murry
An' he's too old fer fancy.
She honly wants free;
She honly wants gone.
But he's plainted,

Roots dug down deep in th' groun'.
Hers comes huncover'd hweth tyears.
His wants become needs
T' wher he culd want
'thout ahartin',

Delicate, pale an' slight,
Plaitin' her mousy brown har,
He passes er by
An' er spur't falls.
Does he gather?

Would he stoop t' pluck grass
T' athreshin in his fiel'?
Would she give him flow'rs
When he wants a chil'?
Hit's s' foolish...

V

Nobody ner nothin's free;
Not you, not me—ever'thang has a price.
Hef everthin has value, hit all costs:

Th' fabric hit hwas made from,
Dyed 'n colored t' be tasted b' eyes,
Warshed t' be felt an' curried t' th' nose.

But ye can't pay off th' cold.
Ye can't buy a human han ner hit's touch,
Th' light that bears th' frame 'f bone through life.

VI

Th' taste 'f fox grapes
Is somethin tween earth an' sky,
Th' way wild grapes grows

As hef they hwas meant
T' be tasted by th' birds
An' creatures that flies,

Squirrels an' chipmunks, too,
Ambrosia 'f th' tree tops,
Nectar 'f th' ar.

Th' juice is night black
An'll stain yer fanger's skin
T' parple an' blue.

VII

I'm a stranger in a strange lan,
Maybe th' stranges 'f lans.
Chapped b' th' wind an' sun
Honly m' body awalkin
Th' breath 'f life in m' chest
Seems t' go t' retarn
M' soul went home t' m' mother,
Who the hell knows fer how long?
Do I belong hyar yet?
M' feet are curious 'n bleed.
I tuck city boy poisons,
Saw God in a moment.
I finally foun love in me
Honly t' want hit given
Away t' somebody.
I give hit in secret, in thought
T' creatures I didn't know,
Lovers I imagined,
Even t' people I despise…
Like last year, I dreamed alone,
I slept in m' casket.
This hisn't a costume I war.
I came hyar 's a stranger
So I culd be mysef.

VIII

Hef I'm th' apern aroun you
Er honly tied t' hit's strangs
Er hef I'm jes a crumb in yer pocket
I'm contented yet t' be thar,

Cause hyou'll fin me jes th' same

I'll be as close as hyou'll allow
Er as scarce as y' requar,
Play hide an' seek er house, play hell fer you
So as I covet yer anger

An' soon as have yer honey.

I've stored hit up b' th' gallons,
An' hwhen you need a lettle,
Brang hit slowly t' yer tarst-whetted mouth
Fer hit t' go inside from out

Till hit glestens on yer chin.

I'll seine hup each collected drip
In th' tout net 'f m' lips,
Not t' keep longer than a nar dyear mem'ry,
But like a songbird 'n yer han,

A tune in a blind man's ears.

IX

An ol' sideways drunk hweth ever jarking narve
Preaches sermons t' whores an' housewives an' boys
An' of ever kin', religion an' creed.

Some lestens between sips 'f coffee
While others tries not t' hyar or t' notice
Th' gurglin, belchin coyote on th' stool.

His life's all t' shit an' his min' is all t' hell
And he laughs at his tyears an' cries at his jokes
Cause th' misery's his an' th' joke is on him.

Th' kindness he shows is offensive an' quar:
Hit's too loud t' lesten, too quiet t' see . . .
Th' most sincere lar in th' whole damn county.

He sleeps on a pallet they made on th' floor
'f gossip, th' half-truths an' gud intentions...
Vain is th' shakin han that holds his last drop.

Did his relevance die hweth a time gone by?
Is his kingdom acomin on clouds that rains?
Can th' wine he dranks be tarned back t' water?

X

Th' cracked an' holy hans
Day hupon night hupon day
Rollin th' rusty, stoney life
T' ever rung 'f Jacob's Ladder
Stare ye in the' face

Demanding hows an' hwhy's,
Expectin ever gud thang
God er earth er person culd give,
Determined t' move in Jesus' Name,
Black-stained an' empty,

Taught in th' way t' go
Carsin 'n blessin, buildin,
Pebbles ripplin th' static cloth
Pushin, pullin th' seen an' unseen,
Recall th' sharp thorn,

Brang t' thought th' tann'd skin
As eyes watch stainless sunset
On th' horizon at ther feet
Whur water trades places hweth th' ar
Fall still t' touch dreams.

XI

Tarn agin leaves t' gray ... t' hwhite.
Splay hup thirsty an' dry,
Shade t' nothin but lighter shade

As hef t' blow th' gentle kiss
That blowed true love away
Fore I culd stoop t' peck hit hup.

Th' strange, quar lesp 'f a promise;
T' hold hit in th' mouth;
T' hwait 'ntil th' taste 's gone!

Senses pushed fer sake 'f lemits,
Th' scent 'f a crayon-box,
A perfume, not 'f a woman

An' warshin powders, a stale scarf
Wadded, ascratchin lak
Thestle hay on that cotton dress.

Col hans akendle a new far.
Th' cowlick, th' parched sweat,
Th' sticky heat 'f, 'I'll not tell'.

Tarn agin leaves t' gray ... silver
Open hup t' th' sky.
Ever yar's winter brangs 'er back.

XII

Does th' jay ever fly low enough
T' see hwhat th' fesh sees,
Or th' trout consider shapes 'f clouds?

Whur wuld th' kangsnake warm by th' far,
Feel th' soaked-in stang 'f snow
On th' fanger or th' cowhide boot?

An' hwhen'll frogs hunt hweth bows an' arr'ws
Fletched hweth th' wangs 'f flies
Pinted hweth th' thorn 'f a locust?

XIII

I've lost m' thread an' needle,
Misplaced th' cushion an' pins.
I culd mend anythin:
A house dress, a pillar,
A hole in th' knee . . .

An' hef you'd agree,
Hef you'd have hit,
A broken soul.
Hit's God's work,
But hweth hep,

I wuld
'n swooft.

Soon;
Soon.

XIV

I did not hunderstan'
An' far too long
Th' song I hyeard
Hweth m' young, stubborn ears:
'Black is th' Color 'f M' True Love's Har'.

Th' senile romantic
Smiles so perverse,
Plucking petals
From hanother lifetime,
A hwhoopperwill warblin in hit's dotage

Sangs hit's own falling dirge,
Hit's love is made
Hit's winding sheet
An' hope becomes hit's grave.
I thought oncet: 'Hwhat a silly way t' die!'

How pintless is th' stang
'f emotion
S' carelessly
Toss'd t' th' tiring grasp
'f a shakin hand cast 'n th' darkness;

Pulled back as hit hwas give,
Hit tarns t' thread,
A web forgot,
An' some poor fly be caught
T' hwether an' t' writhe, t' die fer none.

An' oncet I saw you pass,
I jumped to you
From off th' edge,
Th' concrete paraphet
That kept me safe an' cold hwas proven death.

I'm not afraid t' die
Hef this is life!
An' hef I'm dead,
I'll shorely live again!
You are my naked truth, pale an' tremblin.

Hwhat did sugar taste lak?
Hhwas hit sweeter?
Sticky honey:
Give m' tongue th' answers
An' play yer games on my breath, in my mouth!

Lay hweth me t' leave me,
Let me suffer
Watchin you go.
I am passin away
In a way I can justify stayin.

For you I'll be waitin,
Hwhen th' sun sets,
Wind beaten, sore.
I know now who you are,
By yer touch; by the color 'f yer har.

XV

She till'd th' dart hweth broken glass;
Ther hwas no hanle,
Jest th' blue shards
Hweth ther soft an' sharp edges
Dividin earth from stone

An' th' ivrybone fangerskin
Powder-smerd hweth dust
Lak bee pollen.
Adryin hup fresh-drawn blood
From th' shallow made cuts.

She made th' best 'f hwhat she lack'd
An' had so lettle
That she hwas rich
In kindness an' honesty;
A credit to hersef.

XVI

Considerin th' bards that flies,
T' call t' mind a time when they
hwas salamander thangs,
I cain't be shore 'f how they went,
Ner how they come t' be.

They say that they hwas lizard-like
Hweth feathers jest th' same as now.
Lak people sometimes is
They lived hweth honly selfish greed
Huntil they met ther end.

Hwhatever science says 'f bards,
'f dinosaurs er humankind,
A simple fact remains:
A bard cain't fly hweth jest one wang;
Hit needs both left an' right.

XVII

Playpurties made 'f glass an' porcelain,
Plates an' figurines; crystals an' bulbs,
Painted hweth cobalt bluer than any water,
Rainbow-tinted hweth th' promises
'f a happy lan far, far away.

To possess a man…hit cain't be done
An' who 'f you wuld want t' do it?
We all hold boldly on t' thangs that make us feel
An' savor salt an' all, sweet an' sour;
You ARE a warm-blooded soul aren't you?

Hef you must hold th' dust-worn cases,
Hef you will keep th' laws 'f killers,
Hef you insist t' exist in this made-up game,
The wellsprang 'f Hell man made so well,
Surround yoursef hweth love an' beauty.

XVIII

Millie piles er dark-warshed har
In a twested gaum 'f nightshade,
Occasional shootin white starlight
Intersectin th' strands 'f blue-black,

Pullin ribbon by ribbon
Down t' th' palest soapstone neck,
Th' buttermilk shoulders an' collar,
T' make straight what God made unruly.

Hot-primed copper ir'n an' cord
Defy th' humble holy thread
An' one b' one they're all fallin down;
Rememb'rin t' her th' nurs'ry rhyme.

XIX

Brang me blockade whisky
From th' blue an' parple ridges,
Seal'd in jars 'f glass
Lidded an' banded alak.
M' soul is scorch'd.

Tune an' play th' feddle
Fer a heartbroke, dyin sanger
Propp'd hup fer his end
An' sendin off t' heaven.
Can I leave you?

Let th' one I love best
Place th' kesses 'f an angel,
Th' warmth 'f love's far
That brought me safely to die:
How I'll miss them!

Then sang t' me of heav'n,
Hwhur I have a hope t' travel,
T' live eternal
From th' trespass 'f this clay,
An' let me sleep.

XX

Hef I hwas in m' bottle,
Aroarin through th' neck
From th' clar glass walls
Hwhur I slaked m' brain hwheth drank,
Hwuld hit put you t' shame?

Hef I hwas broke an' finish'd,
Poor as Ol' Job's turkey,
Adoin hwethout
Hweth a rainstorm fer my roof,
Hwuld you not say 'hello'?

An' hef I hwas adyin,
A catfesh on th' bank,
Slimy an' dried hup,
An' rech'd out m' frighten'd han,
Hwuld you kiss me goodby?

XXI

Tell me anythin that comes t' min'
As it comes an' how.
Hit's been a long time
Since I've hyeard news from over thar.

Or, wait! Better yet, an' hef you must,
Tell me one you've told
Before, when hit was
Us two, asmokin cigarettes.

You culd add 'r take away a part
'r add some white lies;
Hit don't make a damn!
I'd jes love to hyear you tell one!

I don't min hef they ain't true atall;
God won't strike you dead
Fer abrangin joy;
Hell! - That's how you tell a story!

XXII

Th' angry young boy,
Colt loaded in han
Fer loss of his love,
Approaches th' one
Who tuck er away.

Hit was s' easy
As asqueezin soft,
Th' trigger, th' grip
"YOU SON OF A BITCH!"
Th' red painted street
Culdn't swaller hit:

Another dead boy,
Much lak th' one
Who fard th' loud shot,
Alayin thar dead
Fer n' more than lust.

Th' one will rest still
In his native lan,
A pine pallet bed
Low t' th' groun
In th' windin sheet
An' suit 'f new clothes.

Th' other'll hang
From th' thirteen winds
'f th' soft white twine 'f
His mother's poor heart
That feels ever' coil.

These daughters 'f men
Afallin lak rain
Wring ther hans an' shake
T' th' ice cold hymns
Lak they had no flesh;
Lak they was jes bones.

Two sons dead an' gone
From three an' still more,
But five stung by death.
Who can retarn them
Back t' th' breath 'f God?

XXIII

Th' wheel come off from th' wagon;
All th' while th' clouds was black,
Aspittin through ther teeth.

Hit's walk back home er persist on
An' ahead t' th' next place
Fer this is none t' stay.

Hef you wait huntil hit passes,
You will never come atall;
Home is a place t' die.

Th' other way is none t' go.
Th' storm is John th' Baptist
An' Jesus Christ is home.

XXIV

At th' mouth 'f th' blue hole sprang
Th' feldspar moss is sour;
A bluetail skink raises hits head
An' lowers hit again
T' give regard t' one
Ahidin hwethin th' ferns.

'Good mornin' an' come play,
Come eat th' flies an' nymphs'.

'I'm bein shy for cartain, cause
Th' cat done got m' tail;
Hit snapp'd an' swaller'd hit whole!'

'Hit's a gud thang yer alive,
But, 'f course yer tail will grow.'

XXV

Take th' anger an' the sadness,
Take th' hart an' disappointments
An' put them all into th' hanle
'f an axe, a wedge, er hammer,
An' put hit all t' work
An' t' advantage.

XXVI

Four strangs, unchang'd
Fer five hun'erd yars,
A figured maple slab
An' strips th' same,
Aholdin hup th' vaulted
Sangin red spruce.
Thes is th' feddle:
Hist'ry 'f melody,
Th' songbook 'f th' dead!

XXVII

Th' old man hain't abotherin nobody,
He's jes afinishin livin out mistakes he's made,
Honly drunk an' always hwas
A picture 'f th' last thang God remembers,
Th' measure 'f a shallow, cool an' easy sprang.

XXVIII

I throw'd m' voice
High an' nigh t' th' treetops,
Hup th' summit,
Down th' ravine.
Th' mountains answer'd back
An' bounc'd th' murmrin song aroun'.
I laugh'd an' tried agin
Before th' decay 'f th varse,
T' outdo myself an' them.
Th' ridges an' th' valleys
Threw hit back jes lak a tommyhawk,
Lak a deflected hunter's arr'w.

XXIX

I've got hit in m' mind
T' be better than you see me.
I'm strong enough t' be broken;
I'm small enough t' grow.

So beat me hweth yer rain;
Warsh th' liquor from m' breath hweth kisses.
Bind m' arms hweth yer tongue.
Fuck m' shoulders hweth yer teeth.

I want t' be yer trouble agin.
I want t' war yer taste on m' face;
Addicted t' you my farst time,
Aknowin I culdn't quit

Aknowin I culdn't get peace
Within er without you,
Be in gud trouble with you
Lak two kids apassin notes in charch.

He doesn't mean anythin t' me
Or th' meanness he brangs hout in me.
Yer my best frien,
Yer my sweet, sof, slutty sick kitten.

Whiskey is m' warst, m' dart.
Yer m' best frien, m' dead end
An' I caught th' eye in yer words
Lak a couple 'f kids misbehavin in charch.

XXX

Asculptin wards fer th' sake 'f soun',
T' feel th' cadence tech th' dart.
I taste th' breaths between th' nouns,
An' wear th' song lak a crown 'f gold.
I barth'd th' wards that forg'd hit,
Dropp'd an' soon forgot.

XXXI

My all an' all,
My ever'thang,
Whur do I go
That ye aren't thar?

Not 'n meanness—
I hid from an'
Hart ye sorely,
Spat ye luke warm
Hwhen ye was hot.

I'd hol' ye now,
Hinto m' neck,
Selfishly so
Hwethout concarn,

Let angels see.
Ye wanted me
T' say th' wards
Ye taught me to.
I never wuld,
Didn' know how.

Now all too late,
I've larnt t' speak
An' hain't fit to.
I'd have ye quick,
But now ye're col'.

www.ingramcontent.com/pod-product-compliance
Lightning Source LLC
Chambersburg PA
CBHW032053290426
44110CB00012B/1064